Sculpting with Clay

Reason with Shapes and Their Attributes

Stella Bienik

PowerKiDS press™

NEW YORK

Published in 2015 by The Rosen Publishing Group, Inc.
29 East 21st Street, New York, NY 10010

Book Design: Mickey Harmon

Photo Credits: Cover Fuse/Thinkstock.com; p. 5 Vyaseleva Elena/Shutterstock.com; p. 7 (main) KhushiAnn/Shutterstock.com; p. 7 (inset) akiyoko/Shutterstock.com; p. 9 Igor A. Bondarenko/Shutterstock.com; pp. 11, 13, 15, 17, 19, 21 (table) colors/Shutterstock.com; pp. 11, 19 (clay) tescha555/Shutterstock.com; pp. 13 (worm), 21 (turtle) warapatrs/Shutterstock.com; p. 15 (star, moon, sun) Bule Sky Studio/Shutterstock.com; p. 17 (raindrops) photka/Shutterstock.com; p. 22 GSPhotography/Shutterstock.com.

Library of Congress Cataloging-in-Publication Data

Bienik, Stella, author.
 Sculpting with clay : reason with shapes and their attributes / Stella Bienik.
     pages cm. — (Math masters. Geometry)
 Includes index.

ISBN 978-1-4777-4906-7 (pbk.)
ISBN 978-1-4777-4907-4 (6-pack)
ISBN 978-1-4777-6444-2 (library binding)

1. Geometry—Juvenile literature. 2. Shapes—Juvenile literature. 3. Modeling—Juvenile literature. [1. Clay modeling.] I. Title.
 QA445.5.B54 2015
 516—dc23

2013049345

Manufactured in the United States of America

CPSIA Compliance Information: Batch #WS15RC: For further information contact Rosen Publishing, New York, New York at 1-800-237-9932.

Contents

An Art Class Sculptor

Art class is my favorite subject in school. We draw, paint, and make things with different **materials**. Today, we're working with clay. I like to work with clay because you can **sculpt** it into whatever shape you'd like.

People who work with clay are called **sculptors**. Some people do this for fun, and others do it as their job. Sculpting with clay during art class makes me a sculptor, too!

> Clay can be messy to work with, but that's what makes it fun!

Clay is fun to work with. Some kinds of clay are dark and brown like mud. Other kinds of clay come in different colors, such as blue, pink, and green.

Clay becomes wet and sticky when you mix it with water. That helps you sculpt it into different shapes. Once you've made a shape, you can bake it to make your object hard and dry. Or you can reshape it into something else.

It's easy to split clay into pieces. It's fun to shape them into different objects.

wet clay

baked clay

Making Shapes with Clay

My teacher says I can make almost anything out of clay. Today, we're making circles and rectangles.

Circles and rectangles can be **divided** into smaller parts, called shares. Each share is the same size. Two equal shares are called halves. Three equal shares are called thirds. Four equal shares are called fourths.

Halves, thirds, and fourths are **fractions**. Equal fractions are the same size, but they don't have to be the same shape.

1 **1 whole**

½ ½ **2 halves**

⅓ ⅓ ⅓ **3 thirds**

¼ ¼ ¼ ¼ **4 fourths**

I sculpt with white clay first. I cut a ball of clay down the middle to make 2 halves. Each half is an equal share of the whole ball of clay. They're equal because they both have the same amount of clay.

I can make 1 of my halves into a cool shape. My clay is white, so I'll make a cloud. Now the halves look different, but they're still equal shares.

If I shape my white cloud into something else, it will still hold the same amount of clay.

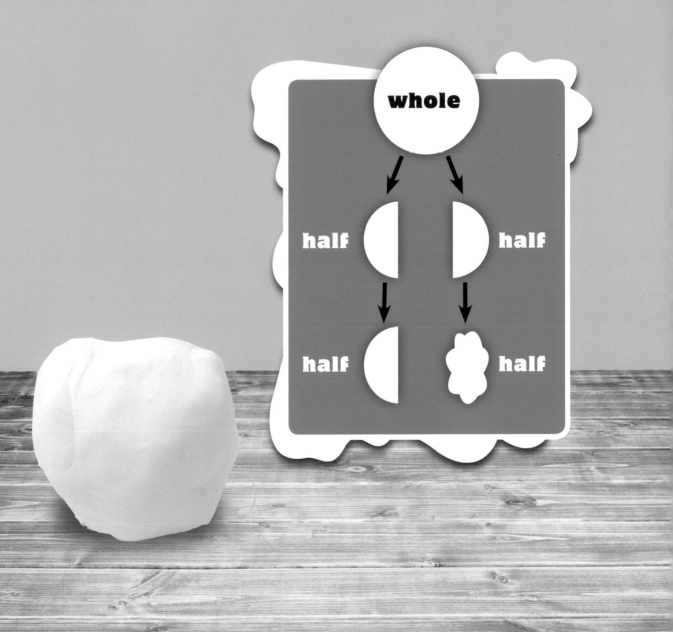

Colorful Clay Shapes

I use green clay next. The green clay is the same size as the white clay I used before. When I cut this clay in half, I make 2 green halves that each have the same amount of clay. They're the same as the white halves, too.

I use 1 half of my green clay to make a worm. The worm looks very different from the cloud, but guess what? They're equal because they're both halves of the same-size whole.

The worm I made doesn't look like the halves I made before. The worm is still made of half of the original ball of clay, though.

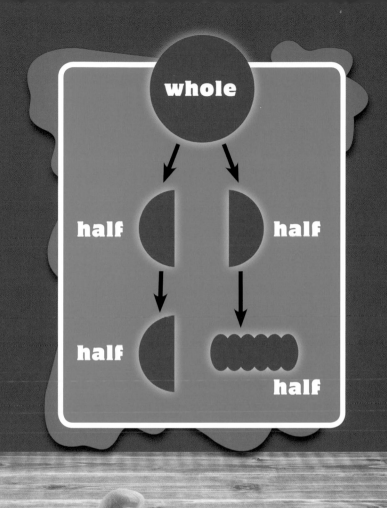

13

Next, my teacher gives me a ball of yellow clay. It's the same size and shape as the green and white clay I used.

I divide the yellow clay into 3 equal shares. They're called thirds. I can make each third into a different shape. I make a star, a moon, and a sun! They look very different, but I know each shape is still a third of the original ball of clay. That makes them equal to each other.

The star, moon, and sun are all equal to each other. However, they're not equal to my worm or my cloud. Those are made of halves, which are bigger than thirds.

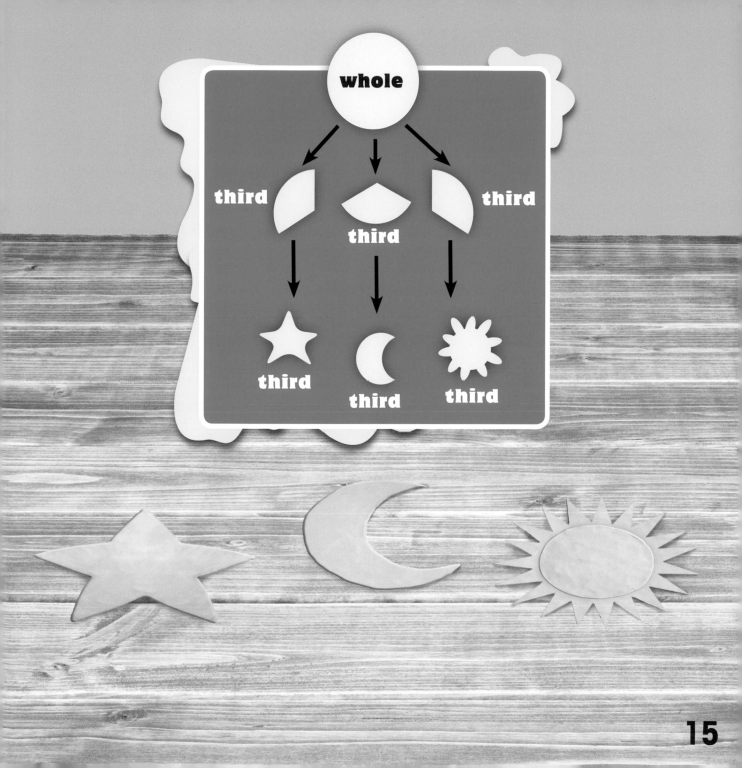

15

I've already made a lot of cool things with my clay, but there are still more colors to use. I use blue next. I'm going to make this clay look like the rain outside.

I cut my blue clay into 2 equal shares. I shape 1 share into a rain cloud. Next, I'll make raindrops. I take the other share and divide it into 20 little pieces. These pieces remind me of the rain outside!

The cloud and the raindrops look very different. It almost looks like the raindrops are made of less clay than the cloud. But I used the same amount for both.

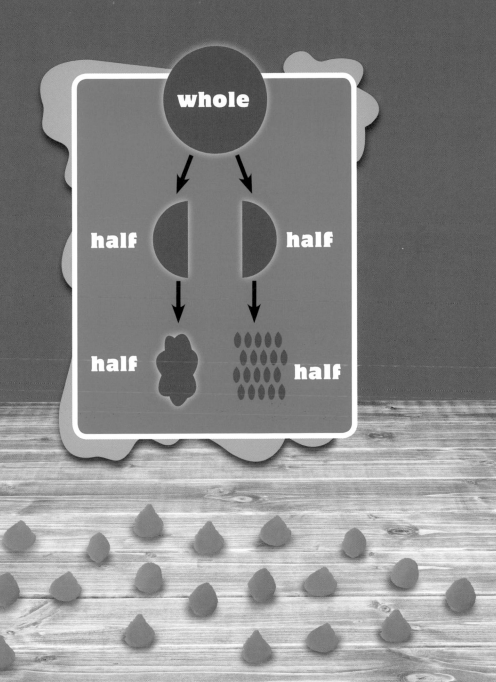

Bill the Turtle

My art teacher tells us to make our favorite animal. My favorite animal is a turtle. I even have a pet turtle named Bill. I'm going to use different-colored clay to make a turtle that looks like him.

Bill has a green body and a colorful shell. His body is pretty big, and his shell covers his whole body. I know I should start with an equal amount of green clay and orange clay.

These balls of clay don't look like much now, but soon, they'll look just like Bill!

green = orange

I make Bill's body first. He has a round, flat body and 4 legs. I flatten some of my green clay into a round shape. Then, I use the rest to make legs and a head. I make a tail, too.

Next, I have to make Bill's shell. His shell lays on his back. I use all my orange clay to make the shell. I think my clay turtle looks just like Bill!

My orange and green clay look very different from what I started with. The body and shell also look different from each other. But guess what? They're still made of equal shares.

21

Time to Clean Up

I know there are many other ways to use my clay. I could try shaping it into people, animals, plants, and more. I can even smash my clay back together to make a whole ball again. I can use different colors to make my shapes look like things I see in the real world.

Soon, art class is over. It's fun to work and sculpt with clay. What do you like to do in art class?

Glossary

divide (duh-VYD) To break into smaller parts or shares.

fraction (FRAK-shun) One of several equal parts into which a whole is divided.

material (muh-TIHR-ee-uhl) Something from which something else can be made.

sculpt (SKUHLPT) To create a solid shape by carving it, casting it, or by using other shaping methods.

sculptor (SKUHLP-tuhr) An artist who makes sculptures.

Index